Melodies for the Craft

Also from Westphalia Press
westphaliapress.org

Melodies for the Craft, or Songs for Freemasons Suitable for Every Occasion

By Jacob Ernst, "A Past Master"

WESTPHALIA PRESS
An Imprint of Policy Studies Organization

Melodies for the Craft, or Songs for Freemasons
Suitable for Every Occasion
All Rights Reserved © 2018 by Policy Studies Organization

Westphalia Press
An imprint of Policy Studies Organization
1527 New Hampshire Ave. NW
Washington, D.C. 20036
info@ipsonet.org

ISBN-13: 978-1-63391-710-1
ISBN-10: 1-63391-710-X

Cover design by Jeffrey Barnes:
jbarnesbook.design

Daniel Gutierrez-Sandoval, Executive Director
PSO and Westphalia Press

Updated material and comments on this edition
can be found at the Westphalia Press website:
www.westphaliapress.org

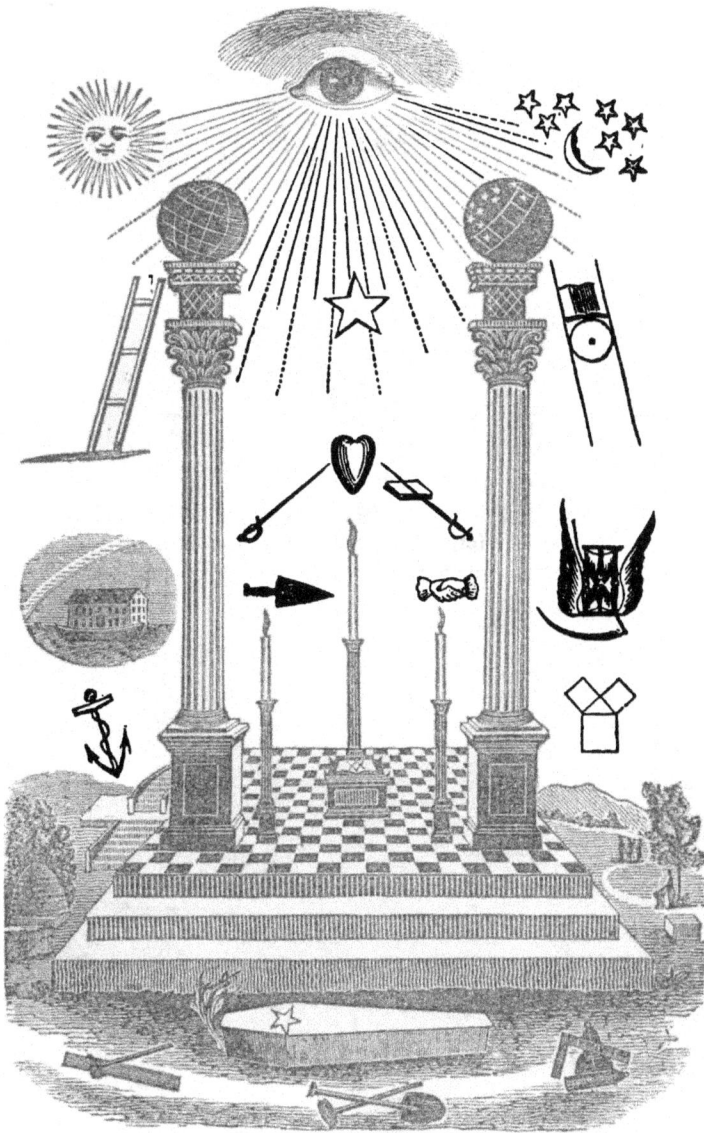

STEREOTYPED BY A. C. JAMES,
167 WALNUT ST., CINCINNATI.

CINCINNATI:
Morgan & Overend, Printers.

MELODIES

FOR THE CRAFT,

OR

SONGS FOR FREEMASONS.

SUITABLE FOR EVERY OCCASION.

Compiled by a Past Master.

CINCINNATI:
JACOB ERNST, 112 MAIN STREET.
1852.

INDEX.

vi   INDEX.

PREFACE.

IF "music hath charms," there is no more appropriate place for it than the Lodge room, and other assemblages of the Craft. Having been many years connected with the Order, the compiler has long been of the opinion that the use of proper melodies in the Lodge room would be productive of much good; for, while it exerts a favorable influence upon the hearts of the members, it begets a love for music and poetry, which of itself is an acquisition.

There are many songs and hymns suitable for every occasion, but they are found scattered through books and magazines, and consequently are difficult of access. It has been thought desirable to have them collected and placed within the reach of all; and the compiler has made an effort, in the work now presented, to accomplish this. He has gathered these from many sources; many of them old and antiquated works, beyond the reach of the great body of Masons. He has also arranged them under suitable heads for various occasions, and accompanied some of the pieces with the music adapted to the words.

If by his labor a single brother shall be made happier or better, he will be amply rewarded for his trouble.

COMPILER.

September, 1852.

MELODIES FOR THE CRAFT.

AT THE OPENING OF A LODGE.

1. INVOCATION.

When from cha - ot - ic sleep, Heav'd up the

When from cha - ot - ic sleep, Heav'd up the

mighty deep   enrob'd in   night ; Then ere Earth's

mighty deep   enrob'd in   night ; Then ere Earth's

beauties woke, His voice the stillness broke, And thus the'Al-

beauties woke, His voice the stillness broke, And thus the'Al-

migh - ty spoke — "Let   there be   Light."

migh - ty spoke — "Let   there be   Light."

Swift from yon orb of day
Fled those dark shades away
        At His dread word ;
Then sang the stars on high,
And through the arching sky
Swelled Heav'n's loud minstrelsy,
        Praise ye the Lord.

Almighty power supreme,
Send down thy brightest beam
        To every heart !
Illume us with thy grace,
Show us thy glorious face,
And Heav'n's own righteousness
        To each impart.

------

2. HYMN.

Blest be the tie, that binds
    Our hearts in virtuous love ;
The fellowship of kindred minds
    Is like to that above.

Before our Father's throne,
    We pour our ardent prayers,
Our fears, our hopes, our aims are one,
    Our comforts and our cares.

We share our mutual woes,
    Our mutual burdens bear ;
And often for each other flows
    The sympathizing tear.

When we asunder part,
    It gives us inward pain ;

But we shall still be join'd in heart,
And hope to meet again.

This glorious hope revives
Our courage by the way;
While each in expectation lives,
And longs to see the day.

3. HYMN.

ALLEGRETTO.

Fa-ther of our fee - ble race,

Fa-ther of our fee - ble race,

Wise, com - pas - sion—Wise, com - pas-

Wise, com - pas - sion—Wise, com - pas-

sion - ate and kind; Spread o'er na-ture's

sion - ate and kind; Spread o'er na-ture's

am - ple face, Flows thy good-ness,

am - ple face, Flows thy good-ness,

Flows   thy   good - ness   un - con-fin'd.

Flows   thy   good - ness   un - con-fin'd.

Mu - sing   in   the   si - lent   grove,

Mu - sing   in   the   si - lent   grove,

Or   the   bu - sy walks   of   men,   Still

Or   the   bu - sy walks   of   men,   Still

we trace thy wond' - rous love,

we trace thy wond' - rous love,

Claim - ing large re - turns a - gain.

Claim - ing large re - turns a - gain.

Lord, what off 'ring shall we bring
   At thine Altar, when we bow;
Hearts, the pure, unsullied spring,
   Whence the kind affections flow.
Soft compassion's feeling soul,
   By the melting eye express'd;
Sympathy, at whose control,
   Sorrow leaves the wounded breast.

Willing hands to lead the blind,
   Bind the wounded, feed the poor;

Love, embracing all mankind,
  Charity, with liberal store.
Teach us, O thou heav'nly King,
  Thus to show our grateful mind ;
Thus th' accepted off'ring bring,
  Love to Thee, and all mankind.

---

4. SONG.

By Masons' art, th' aspiring domes,
  In stately columns shall arise ;
All climates are their native homes,
  Their well-judged actions reach the skies ;
Heroes and kings revere their name,
While poets sing their lasting fame.

Great, noble, gen'rous, good, and brave,
  Are titles they most justly claim ;
Their deeds shall live beyond the grave,
  Which those unborn shall loud proclaim ;
Time shall their generous acts enroll,
While love and friendship charm the soul.

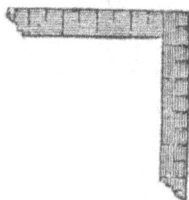

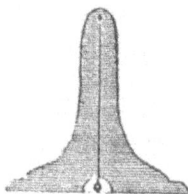

5. ODE.

ANDANTE.

When earth's foun - da - tion first was laid, By

the Al - migh - ty Art-ist's hand,

'Twas then our perfect, our perfect laws were made,

2

Es - tab-lish'd   by   his strict command.

CHORUS.

PIA.

Hail ! myster'ous,   hail, glor'ous Masonry ;

Hail !   myster'ous,   hail   glor'ous Masonry ;

That makes us   ev - er great and free

That makes us   ev - er great and free.

Repeat for.

In vain mankind for shelter sought,
  In vain from place to place did roam,
Until from heaven — from heaven he was taught
  To plan, to build, and fix his home.
          Hail! mysterious, &c.

Illustrious, hence, we date our art,
  Our works in beauteous piles appear;
Which shall to endless — to endless time impart,
  How worthy and how great we are.
          Hail! mysterious, &c.

Nor we less fam'd for ev'ry tie,
  By which the human thought is bound;
Love, truth, and friendship, and friendship socially,
  Join all our hearts and hands around,
          Hail! mysterious, &c.

Our actions still by virtue blest,
  And to our precepts ever true,
The world admiring — admiring, shall request
  To learn, and our bright paths pursue.
          Hail! mysterious, &c.

---

6. SONG.

Genius of Masonry, descend,
  And with thee bring thy spotless train;
Constant our sacred rites attend,
  While we adore thy peaceful reign;
Bring with thee Virtue, brightest maid,
  Bring love, bring truth, bring friendship here;
While social mirth shall lend her aid,
  To smooth the wrinkled brow of care.

Come Charity, with goodness crown 'd,
  Encircled in thy heavenly robe,
Diffuse thy blessings all around,
  To every corner of the globe.
See where she comes, with power to bless,
  With open hand and tender heart,
Which, wounded, feels at man's distress,
  And bleeds at every human smart.

Envy may every ill devise,
  And falsehood be thy deadliest foe ;
Thou, friendship, still shalt towering rise,
  And sink thine adversaries low :
Thy well-built pile shall long endure,
  Through rolling years preserve its prime,
Upon a rock it stands secure,
  And braves the rude assaults of time.

Ye happy few, who here extend
  In perfect lines, from east to west,
With fervent zeal the lodge defend,
  And lock its secrets in each breast :
Since ye are met upon the square,
  Bid love and friendship jointly reign,
Be peace and harmony your care,
  Nor break the adamantine chain.

Behold the planets how they move,
  Yet keep due order as they run ;
Then imitate the stars above,
  And shine resplendent as the sun :
That future Masons, when they meet,
  May all our glorious deeds rehearse,
And say, their fathers were so great,
  That they adorn 'd the universe.

7. SONG.

ANDANTINO.

Thus hap - pi - ly met, u - ni - ted and free, A foretaste of heav - en we prove

For. Then join heart and hand and firmly agree,

Pia. Then join heart and hand and firm - ly a - gree

For. To cul - ti - vate bro-ther - ly love.

With corn, wine, and oil, our table replete,
  The Altar of friendship divine ;
Each virtue and grace to the circle complete,
  While wreaths of pure song we entwine.

Thus blest and thus blessing in work so supreme,
  May Masonry daily increase ;
Its grand scheme of morals, our favorite theme
  The source of contentment and peace.

8. ODE.

Here *Wisdom* her standard displays,
　　Here nobly the sciences shine ;
Here the Temple's vast column we raise,
　　And finish a work that's divine,
Illum'd from the *East* with pure light,
　　Here arts do their blessings bestow ;
And all perfect unfold to the sight
　　What none but a Mason can know.

With *fervency, freedom,* and *zeal,*
　　Our Master's commands we obey ;
No cowan our secrets can steal,
　　No babbler our myst'ries betray,
Here all competitions must cease —
　　Of discord not even one strain
Disturbs e'er the Lodge's sweet peace,
　　Where *silence* and *harmony* reign.

If on earth any praise can be found,
　　Any virtue unnam'd in my song,
Any grace in the Universe round,
　　May these to a Mason belong !
May each Brother his passions subdue,
　　Practice *Charity, Concord,* and *Love ;*
And be hail'd by the thrice happy few
　　Who preside in the Grand Lodge above.

9. ODE.

ALLEGRETTO. Mezzo for.

What joy, when brethren dwell com-

Instrumental.

Pia.

bin'd, In - spir - ing u - ni - ty of

mind ; 'Tis like the sacred unc — tion

shed   on Aaron's   ven - er - a - ble   head;

When bath'd   in   fra - gran - cy   re-

spire   His   rev - 'rend   beard   and

rich at - tire, His rev - 'rend

beard and rich at - tire.

Like dews, which, trickling from the sky,
In pearly drops on Hermon lie ;
Or balmy vapors which distill
On Zion's consecrated hill ;
For there the Lord his blessing plac'd,
And these with life eternal grac'd.

10. SONG.

Come, Brothers of the mystic tie—
Our social work begun —
We'll raise an offering song on high,
To him the Holy One.

Chorus—With hearts united firm and free,
We round our Altar stand ;
Who best can work and best agree,
Are dearest in our band.

Come kindle at our holy fire,
Fraternal thoughts and kind ;
Each worthy act and pure desire
Shall kindred wishes bind.

Chorus—With hearts united, firm and free,
We round our altar stand ;
Who best can work, and best agree,
Are dearest in our band.

---

11. SONG.

Unite, unite, your voices raise ;
Loudly sing Free-masons' praise :
Spread far and wide their spotless **fame**,
And glory in the sacred name.

Behold, behold, the upright band
In virtue's paths go hand in hand ;
They shun each ill, they do no **wrong**,
Strict honor does to them belong.

How just, how just, are all their ways!
Superior far to mortal praise;
Their worth description far exceeds,
For matchless are Free-masons' deeds.

Go on, go on, ye just and true,
And still the same bright paths pursue;
Th' admiring world shall on ye gaze,
And friendship's altar ever blaze.

Begone, begone, fly discord hence!
With party rage and insolence!
Sweet peace shall bless this happy band,
And freedom smile throughout the land.

---

12.   SONG.

HAIL Masonry! thou Art divine;
Come, brethren! let us cheerful join
To celebrate this happy day,
And homage to our Master pay.

Hail! happy, blest and sacred place!
Where friendship brightens every face
Where mystic Art adorns the chair,
Resplendent with his upright square.

Next sing, my muse, our Warden's praise,
With chorus loud in tuneful lays;
Oh! may these columns ne'er decay,
Until the world dissolves away.

My brethren cheerful, join with me,
To sing the praise of Masonry:
The noble, faithful, and the brave,
Whose art shall live beyond the grave.

13. ODE.

BEHOLD ! how pleasant, and how good,
 For brethren, such as we,
Of the " Accepted " brotherhood,
 To dwell in unity !
'T is like the oil on Aaron's head
 Which to his feet distills ;
Like Hermon's dew so richly shed
 On Zion's sacred hills.

For there the Lord of light and love,
 A blessing sent with power ;
Oh, may we all this blessing prove,
 E'en life for evermore ;
On Friendship's altar rising here
 Our hands now plighted be,
To live in *love* with hearts sincere,
 In *peace* and *unity.*

AT THE CLOSING OF A LODGE

14. HYMN.

Great Ar-chi-tect ! Supreme, di - vine,

Great Ar-chi-tect ! Su-preme, di - vine,

Whose wisdom plann'd the grand de - sign,

Whose wisdom plann'd the grand de - sign,

And gave to na - ture birth;

And gave to na - ture birth;

Pia.

Whose word with light a - dorn'd the skies,

Whose word with light a - dorn'd the skies,

Gave mat - ter form, bade or - der rise,

Gave mat - ter form, bade or - der rise,

And bless 'd the new - born earth :

And bless 'd the new - born earth :

CHORUS.

'Till love shall cease, 'till or - der dies,

'Till love shall cease 'till or - der dies,

To Thee ma - son - ic praise shall rise.

To Thee ma - son - ic praise shall rise.

O, bless this love-cemented band,
Form'd and supported by thy hand,
   For Charity's employ;
To shield the wretched from despair,
To spread through scenes of grief and care,
   Reviving rays of joy.
Chorus — 'Till love, &c.

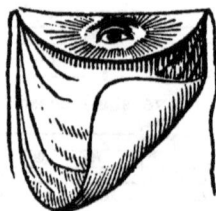

The lib'ral Arts, by Thee design'd,
To polish, comfort, aid mankind,
   We labor to improve ;
While we adore Jehovah's name,
Pour on our hearts the melting flame,
   And mold our souls to love.
Chorus — 'Till love, &c.

15. DUETT.

NO, NEVER SHALL MY SOUL FORGET.

No, never shall my soul forget
  The friends I found so cordial-hearted;
Dear, dear shall be the day we met,
  And dear shall be the night we parted

Oh, if regrets, however sweet,
  Must with the lapse of time decay;
Yet still, when thus in love you meet,
  Remember him that's far away.

Long be the flame of memory found
  Alive within your social band;
Let that be still the magic round,
  On which oblivion dares not stand.

---

16. SONG.

Sweet is the mem - 'ry   of   the   night,

When first we saw the se - cret light;

Dear to our souls shall ev - er be

The mys - ter - ies of Ma - son - ry.

Grateful to thee our hearts we bend,
O Masonry, the poor man's friend;
Dark through the stream of life must flow,
That it still rolls to thee we owe.

O we have try'd thee, try'd thee long,
When hope had fled, when hope was strong,
Brighter than all our fancy dream'd,
The true, unfading love has beam'd.

Science may shoot its bright, cold ray
Across the pilgrim's painful way:

Honor may plant the laurel there,
For fortune to usurp and wear:

Vain is their pow 'r to warm, O Art,
The chill that settles round the heart;
Thou canst alone beguile the hours,
And strew our rugged way with flow 'rs.

17. ODE.

Hail ! sa - cred art ! by heav'n de - sign'd

Hail ! sa - cred art ! by heav'n de - sign'd

A gra - cious bless - ing for man - kind ;

A gra - cious bless - ing for man - kind ;

Peace, joy, and love thou dost be - stow, On

Peace, joy, and love thou dost be-

us thy vo - ta - ries be - low. Bright

stow, On us thy votaries be - low. Bright

wisdom's footsteps here we trace, From Sol - o-

wisdom's footsteps here we trace,

mon, from Sol-o-mon, from

From Sol - o - mon, from Sol - o - mon,

Sol - o - mon, the prince of peace,

Sol - o - mon, the prince of peace,

Whose righteous maxims still we hold

Whose righteous maxims still we hold

More precious than rich Ophir's gold.

More precious than rich Ophir's gold.

His heav'nly proverbs to us tell,
How we on earth should ever dwell;
In harmony and social love,
To emulate the blest above;
Now having wisdom for our guide,
By its sweet precepts we'll abide;
Nor from its path we'll ever stray,
'Till we shall meet in endless day.

Vain, empty grandeur shall not find.
Its dwelling in a brother's mind;
A Mason, who is true and wise,
Its glittering pomp we'll e'er despise;
Candor, friendship, joy, and peace,
Within his breast shall have a place;
Virtue and wisdom thus combin'd,
Shall decorate the Mason's mind,

18. SONG.

THE MASON'S ADIEU.

Adieu, a heart's warm, fond adieu, dear brethren
Ye favor'd and enlighten'd few, Companions

of the mystic tie, Tho' I to foreign lands must
of my social joy,

hie, Pursuing fortune's slippery ball, With melting

heart and brimful eye, I'll mind you still tho' far awa'.

Oft I have met your social band,
    To spend a cheerful festive night,
.Oft honor'd with supreme command,
    Presiding o'er the sons of light;
And by that hieroglyphic bright,
    Which none but craftsmen ever saw,
Strong mem'ry on my heart shall write,
    Those happy scenes when far awa'.

May freedom, harmony, and love,
    Cement you in the grand design,

Beneath th' Omniscient Eye above,
    That glorious Architect divine ;
That you may keep th' unerring line,
    Still guided by the plummet's law,
'Till order bright completely shine,
    Shall be my prayer when far awa'.

And you, farewell, whose merits claim,
    Justly that highest badge to wear,
May heaven bless your noble name,
    To Masonry and friendship dear :
My last request, permit me then,
    When yearly you're assembled a',
One round, I ask it with a tear,
    To him your friend that's far awa'.

And you, kind-hearted sisters fair,
    I sing farewell to all your charms,
Th' impression of your pleasing air
    With rapture oft my bosom warms.
Alas ! the social winter's night
    No more returns while breath I draw,
'Till sisters, brothers, all unite,
    In that grand Lodge that's far awa'.

---

19. SONG.

THE FAREWELL.

Oh ! it came on the ear like the last solemn warning,
    That breaks the rude slumber of misery's rest,
When the dreams of those joys we must leave in the
        morning,
For a moment gives balm to the bosom unblest.

Could it steal o'er the senses like that Theban
    potion,
  Which curdles the mem'ry and deadens the brain;
Or wither the thought in its saddest emotion,
  Or an antidote bring to the acme of pain.

Could it blight like the Syrian blast, we might
    sever
  With one deadly pang from those friends we love
    best,
And sleep in oblivion, forgetting forever,
  Those eyes that have blest us, those hearts we
    have pressed.

But it comes like the death-peal of hope — and no
    longer
  The glittering visions we 've cherished, beguile;
And its deep cheering tones to impress it the stronger,
  Will oftentimes die on a fugitive smile.

Hath pleasure no charm — and diversion no glad-
    ness,
  To soothe, if not banish, the pain of the past:
Can not time, as it wears, lull the memory's sadness,
  Or soften those sorrows that canker so fast?

Oh no! when we part, recollection will borrow,
  Past touches of bliss, but to quicken the sore;
Those eyes shall be bright that shall meet on the
    morrow,
  Those hearts shall be sad that shall never meet
    more.

20. SONG.

WE met in love, we part in peace,
Our council labors o'er;
We'll ask ere life's best days shall cease,
To meet in time once more.

CHORUS—'Mid fairest scenes to memory dear,
In change of joy and pain;
We'll think of friends assembled here,
And hope to meet again.

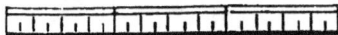

Though changes mark time's onward way
In all we fondly claim,
Fraternal hopes shall ne'er decay—
Our landmarks still the same.

CHORUS—'Mid fairest scenes to memory dear, &c.

Our faith unmoved, with truth our guide,
As seasons mark our clime;
Through winter's chill, or summer's pride,
We'll hail the Art Sublime.

CHORUS—'Mid fairest scenes to memory dear, &c.

When life shall find its silent close,
With hopes kind promise blest;
In that Grand Lodge may all repose,
Where joys immortal rest.

CHORUS—'Mid fairest scenes to memory dear,
In change of joy and pain;
We'll think of friends assembled here,
And hope to meet again.

21. SONG.

STILL tell my heart of heavenly peace,
　And let my quickened fancy soar,
To realms where every doubt shall cease,
　And our freed spirits part no more.

This truth divine our souls shall charm,
　And holy peace and joy restore;
Afar from sorrow and alarm,
　We all shall meet to part no more.

O, in that word there is a spell
　·Sinks to my bosom's inmost core;
For here on earth we hear the knell
　Of fondest friends who meet no more.

Then may we hope in heaven to meet,
　When all Time's woes and strifes are o'er,
To find at last a sure retreat,
　Where our glad hearts shall part no more.

ENTERED APPRENTICE SONGS.

22. SONG

In whom may we trust ? Shall the buckler of power
Be the aid of the heart in adversity's hour ?
Shall we lean on the hilt of the warrior's sword,
Or trust on the breath of a sovereign's word ?
The sword may be snapp'd, or the mighty one's breath,
Be chilled ere its promise is plighted in death !
And hopes which were springing to brighten our way,
Fall back on the heart in woes darkest array.

But were there a being in whom all combin'd,
Power, wisdom and love — some omnipotent mind,
Which all things foreseeing, could all things prevent,
Or mold into mercy the coming event —
There, there might the spirit with safety confide,
For power to assist, and for wisdom to guide ;
For love to support till the *rough path* be trod,
Then, pilgrim, look upward — *that being is God.*

23. SONG.

"LET there be light," the first command,
  That burst from heav'n's exalted throne!
Jehovah gave the stern decree,
  And forth immediate radiance shone.

The sun, that glorious orb of day,
  Was order'd to assume his sphere;
To shed on earth th' enliv'ning ray,
  To shine abroad from year to year.

But there's a light, a brighter light,
  Than sun or nature e'er could claim;
'T is shed through all creation's space,
  And bears a great and glorious name.

This light has shone since man was born,
  And will e'er shine till worlds decay;
Its brightness far exceeds the morn,
  With it the gloomy night is day.

Then let us search for this great Light,
  Which shines with such refulgence broad;

From scorching heat and piercing cold,
  From beasts, whose roar the forest rends;
From the assaults of warriors bold,
  The Mason's art mankind defends.
    Be to this art due honor paid,
    From which mankind receives such aid.

Ensigns of state, that feed our pride,
  Distinctions troublesome and vain,
By Masons true are laid aside,
  Art's free-born sons such toys disdain;
    Ennobled by the name they bear,
    Distinguish'd by the badge they wear.

Sweet fellowship, from envy free,
  Friendly converse of brotherhood,
The lodge's lasting cement be,
  Which has for ages firmly stood.
    A lodge thus built, for ages past
    Has lasted, and shall ever last.

Then let us celebrate the praise
  Of all who have enrich'd the art,
Let gratitude our voices raise,
  And each true brother bear a part.
    Let cheerful strains their fame resound,
    And living Masons' healths go round.

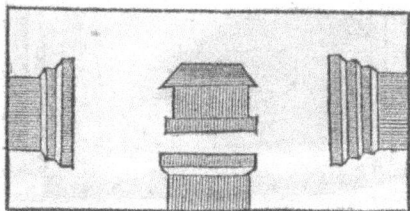

27. ODE.

Come, Craftsmen, assembled our pleasure to share,
Who walk by the Plumb, and who work by the Square;
While traveling in love, on the Level of time,
Sweet hope shall light on to a far better clime

We'll seek, in our labors, the Spirit Divine,
Our temple to bless, and our hearts to refine;
And thus to our altar a tribute we'll bring,
While, joined in true friendship, our anthem we sing.

See Order, and Beauty, rise gently to view,
Each brother a column, so perfect and true!
When Order shall cease, and when temples decay,
May each, fairer columns, immortal, survey.

MASTER MASON'S SONGS.

27. SONG.

Hail! mysterious, glorious science, Hail! mys-

Hail! mys-

terious, glorious science, Hail! mysterious, glorious

terious, glorious science, Hail! mysterious, glorious

science, Which to dis-cord   bids defiance, Harmo-

science, Which to dis-cord   bids defiance, Harmo-

ny alone reigns here, Har-mo-ny alone reigns

ny alone reigns here, Har-mo-ny alone reigns

Mezzo For.

Here.   Come let's sing -   -   -   -

Here.   Come let's sing to Him that

To the

rais 'd us From the rugged path, that maz 'd us, To the

Light, that we re - vere, To the Light, that we re-

Light, that we re - vere, To the Light, that we re-

vere.   Hail, mysterious,

vere.   Hail, mysterious,

glorious science,

Hail, mysterious, Hail, mysterious

Hail, mysterious, Hail, mysterious

glorious science

glorious science, Which to dis-cord gives de-

glorious science, Which to dis-cord gives de-

fi - ance, Har - mo - ny a - lone reigns here,

fi - ance, Har - mo - ny a - lone reigns here,

For.

Har - mo - ny a - - lone reigns here.

Har - mo - ny a - - lone reigns here.

28. DIRGE.

Solemn strikes the funeral chime,

Notes of our de - part - ing time;

As we journey here be - low,

Through a pil - gri - mage of wo!

Mortals, now indulge a tear,
For mortality is near!
See how wide her trophies wave
O 'er the slumbers of the grave!

Here another guest we bring,
Seraphs of celestial wing,
To our funeral altar come,
Waft this Friend and Brother home.

Lord of all! below — above —
Fill our hearts with Truth and Love;
When dissolves our earthly tie,
Take us to thy Lodge on high.

29 SONG.

I SING the Mason's glory,
  Whose praying mind doth burn ;
Unto complete perfection,
  Our mysteries to learn ;
Not those who visit Lodges
  To eat and drink their fill ;
Not those who at our meetings
  Hear lecture ' gainst their will :

The faithful worthy Brother,
  Whose heart can feel for grief ;
Whose bosom with compassion
  Steps forth to his relief,
Whose soul is ever ready,
  Around him to diffuse,
The principles of Masons,
  And guard them from abuse ;

King Solomon, our patron,
  Transmitted this command,
" The faithful and praise-worthy,
  True light must understand ;
And my descendants, also,
  Who 're seated in the *East,*
Have not fulfill 'd their duty,
  ' Till light has reach 'd the *West.*"

My duty and my station,
  As Master in the chair
Obliges me to summon
  Each Brother to prepare ;
That all may be enabled,
  By slow, though sure degrees,
To answer in rotation,
  With honor and with ease.

30. ODE.

Let us remember in our youth,
  Before the evil days draw nigh,
Our Great Creator, and his Truth!
  Ere memory fail, and pleasure fly;
Or sun, or moon, or planet's light
  Grow dark, or clouds return in gloom;
Ere vital spark no more incite;
  When strength shall bow, and years consume.

Let us in youth remember Him!
  Who formed our frame, and spirits gave,
Ere windows of the mind grow dim,
  Or door of speech obstructed wave;
When voice of bird fresh terrors wake;
  And Music's daughters charm no more,
Or fear to rise, with trembling shake,
  Along the path we travel o'er.

In youth, to God let memory cling,
  Before desire shall fail, or wane,
Or e'er he loosed life's silver string,
  Or bowl at fountain rent in twain.
For man to his long home doth go,
  And mourners group around his urn;
Our dust, to dust again must flow,
  And spirits unto God return.

————

31. SONG.

Ah, when shall we three meet like them,
Who last were at Jerusalem;
For three there were, and one is not —
He lies where cassia marks the spot.

Tho' poor he was, with kings he trod;
Tho' great, he humbly knelt to God:
Ah when shall those restore again,
The broken link of Friendship's chain!

Behold where mourning beauty bent
In silence o'er his monument,
And widely spread in sorrow there,
The ringlets of her flowing hair.

The future sons of grief shall sigh,
While standing round in mystic tie,
And raise their hands, alas! to heaven,
In anguish that no hope is given.

From whence we came, or whither go,
Ask me no more, nor seek to know,
'Till three shall meet, who form'd like them,
The Grand Lodge at Jerusalem.

32. SONG.

Mark Mas - ters all ap-pear be-fore the

Mark Mas - ters all ap - pear be-fore the

Chief O'erseer, In con-cert move ;   Let him your

Chief O'erseer, In con-cert move ;   Let him your

work inspect for the chief Architect; if there be

work inspect for the chief Architect; if there be

no de - fect, He will ap - prove.

no de - fect, He will ap - prove.

You have pass'd the square,
For your rewards prepare.
    Join heart and hand ;
Each with his mark in view,
March with the just and true;
Wages to you are due
    At your command.

Hiram, the widow's son,
Sent unto Solomon
    Our great key-stone ;

On it appears the name
Which raises high the fame
Of all to whom the same
    Is truly known.

Now to the westward move,
Where full of strength and love,
    Hiram doth stand;
But if impostors are
Mix'd with the worthy there,
Caution them to beware
    Of the right hand.

Now to th' praise of those
Who triumphed o'er the foes
    Of mason's art;
To the praiseworthy three,
Who founded this degree;
May all their virtues be
    Deep in our hearts.

----

33. ODE.

When all was in chaos before the creation,
    Confusion and darkness prevailed oe'r the deep,
Until the loud voice of the Lords proclamation,
    Bade science arise from her long dormant sleep;
She obey'd the command, and arose in bright splendor,
    Bade darkness avaunt, and light speed the way;
Array'd in full glory, due homage to render,
    Unfurl'd the broad banner and hailed the new day.

The sound of her gavel roused Genius, her hand-maid,
    Who instant came forth, with the compass and
    square;

The plumb-line and level, the chisel and mallet,
  The work of the craftsman to cut and prepare.
Then rally brave craftsmen in bonds of true friendship;
  Behold the fair Temple of Wisdom arise,
Let each faithful brother support one another,
  Till the Lodge universal shall meet in the skies.

34. SONG.

Solo.--Vivace.

At-ten - tion Mark Master you're called to ap-

pear Be-fore our fam'd workmen the chief o - ver

seer, Since our la - bors are fin-ish'd for

wa - ges pre - pare,   The Lord of the

vine-yard,   will   give each his   share.

In concert then move while brotherly love Ex-

pands each warm heart with fire from a - bove.

TRIO.

Exhibit your work then if clear of defect,   It

Exhibit your work then if clear of defect,   It

merits   re - ward from the chief architect.

merits   re - ward from the chief architect.

Mark well every craftsman whose jewel is bright,
If his task is well finished he will him requite;
Each keeping his eye on the *mark* we've in view,
We'll firmly march on with the just and the true.
      Then join heart and hand,
       'Tis your's to command
The reward of your merit, so make your demand;
Exhibit your work, for if clear from defect,
You merit reward from the chief architect.

The widow's son, Hiram,* the key-stone did bring,
To God's own anointed, the Great Hebrew King;
On it may be found what exalts high our fame,
If rightly decyphered, a mystical name.
      The chief architect
      Did this key-stone inspect;
And approved of the same, for 'twas free from
    defect;
Exhibit your work, then, for wages prepare,
The Lord of the vineyard will pay each his share.

In the west stands a brother, who will represent,
That fam'd skilful architect, he who it sent,
But while in his office he thus takes his stand,
Beware all impostors, how you stretch your hand;
      Be cautious, reflect,
      You have cause to expect,
'Tis his business, impostors and cowan's to detect,
Then display your own work, to deceive him do'nt
    dare,
Or in paying the craft you'll receive a just share.

Let posterity e'er bless the names of the three,
Who founded and handed to us this degree:
May their firmness and virtue, by us be enjoyed,

---

* Kings, chapter 7, verse 14.
5

While this world is our Lodge, and we're therein
    employed ;
        Our efforts should be,
        Who best may agree,
And receive from his master the highest degree,
Well remembering if we dont fail to prepare,
The Lord of the vineyard will pay us our *share.*

PAST MASTERS SONGS.

35. HYMN.

FOR INSTALLATION.

Unto Thee, great God! belong   Mystic

Unto Thee great God! belong   Mystic

rites and sacred song; Lowly bending at thy

rites and sa-cred song; Lowly bending at thy

shrine, We hail thy majesty divine.

shrine, We hail thy majesty divine.

Glorious Architect above,
Source of light and source of love;
Here thy light and love prevail,
Hail! Almighty Master hail!

Whilst in yonder regions bright,
The sun by day, the moon by night;
And the stars that gild the sky,
Blazon forth thy praise on high.

Join Oh Earth ; and as you roll
From east to west, from pole to pole,
Lift to HIM your grateful lays,
Join the universal praise.

Warm'd by benignant grace,
Friendship linked the human race :
Pity lodg'd within the breast,
Charity became her guest.

There the naked, raiment found ;
Sickness, balsam for its wound
Sorrow, comfort ; hunger, bread
Strangers, there a welcome shed.

Still to us, O God ! dispense
Thy divine benevolence ;
Teach the tender tear to flow,
Melting at a Brother's woe.

Like Samaria's son, that we,
Blest with boundless charity,
To th' admiring world may prove,
They dwell in God, who dwell in love.

36. SONG.

Let Masonry from pole to pole, Her sacred

Let Masonry from pole to pole, Her sacred

laws expand, Far as the mighty waters roll, To

laws expand, Far as the mighty waters roll, To

wash remotest land, To wash remotest

wash remotest land To wash remotest

land : That virtue has not left mankind, Her

land : That virtue has not left mankind, Her

social maxims prove, For stamp'd upon the

social maxims prove, For stamp'd upon the

Mason's mind, Are u-ni - ty and love, Are

Mason's mind, Are u-ni - ty and love, Are

u – ni – ty and love.

u – ni – ty and love

Ascending to her native sky,
   Let Masonry increase;
A glorious pillar rais'd on high,
   Integrity its base.
Peace adds to olive boughs entwin'd,
   An emblematic dove,
And stamp'd upon the Mason's mind,
   Is unity and love.

MOST EXCELLENT MASTER'S SONG.

37. SONG.

All hail to the morning, That bids us re-

All hail to the morning, That bids us re-

joice; The temple's completed, Exalt high each voice;

joice; The temple's completed, Exalt high each voice;

The capstone is finish'd, Our la - bor is o 'er;

The capstone is finish'd, Our la - bor is o 'er;

The sound of the ga-vel shall hail us no more,

The sound of the ga-vel shall hail us no more,

For.

To the Power Almighty, who ever has gui - ded

To the Power Almighty, who ever has gui - ded

The tribes of old Israel, ex - alt-ing their fame;

The tribes of old Israel, ex - alt-ing their fame;

To Him, who hath govern'd our hearts un-di - vided,

To Him, who hath govern'd our hearts un-di - vided,

Fortiss.

Let's send forth our voices to praise his great Name.

Let's send forth our voices to praise his great Name.

Companions assemble
  On this joyful day;
The occasion is glorious,
  The key-stone to lay:
Fulfill'd is the promise,
  By the ANCIENT OF DAYS,
To bring forth the cap-stone
  With shouting and praise.

[*Ceremonies.*]

There is no more occasion for level or plumb-line,
For trowel or gavel, for compass or square;
Our works are completed, the ark safely seated,
And we shall be greeted as workmen most rare.

Now those who are worthy,
  Our toils who have shar'd,
And prov'd themselves faithful,
  Shall meet their reward;
Their virtue and knowledge,
  Industry and skill,
Have our approbation,
  Have gain'd our good will.

We accept and receive them, Most Excellent Masters,
Invested with honors, and power to preside;
Among worthy crafts-men, wherever assembled,
The knowledge of Masons to spread far and wide.

ALMIGHTY JEHOVAH!
  Descend now and fill
This Lodge with thy glory,
  Our hearts with good will
Preside at our meetings,
  Assist us to find
True pleasure in teaching
  Good will to mankind.

Thy *wisdom* inspired the great institution,
Thy *strength* shall support it till nature expire;
And when the creation shall fall into ruin,
Its *beauty* shall rise through the midst of the fire!

ROYAL ARCH SONGS.

38. SONG.

ALMIGHTY Sire! our heavenly king,
    Before whose sacred name we bend,
Accept the praises which we sing,
    And to our humble prayer attend!
        All hail great Architect divine!
        This universal frame is thine.

Thou who didst Persia's King command,
    A proclamation to extend,
That Israel's sons might quit his land,
    Their holy temple to attend.
        All hail, &c.

That sacred place where three in one,
    Compris'd thy comprehensive name;
And where the bright meridian sun
    Was soon thy glory to proclaim.
        All hail, &c.

---

39. SONG.

Adante Maestoso.

When   orient Wisdom beam'd se - rene, And

pillar'd Strength a - rose; When Beauty ting'd the

glow - ing scene, And Faith her mansion chose; Ex-

ulting bands the fabric view'd, Mysterious powers a-

dor'd; And high the Triple Union stood, And

high the Triple   Union stood, That gave the *mystic*

word, - - - That gave the *mystic* word, - - and

high the Triple   Union stood, That gave the *mystic* word.

Pale envy wither'd at the sight,
    And frowning at the pile,
Call'd murder from the realms of night,
    To blast the glorious toil;
With ruffian outrage, join'd in woe,
    They form the league abhorr'd,
And wounded Science felt the blow,
    That crush'd the *mystic* word.

Concealment, from sequester'd grave,
    On sable pinions flew,

And o 'er the sacrilegious grave,
  Her vail impervious threw ;
Th' associate band in solemn state,
  The awful loss deplor 'd,
And Wisdom mourn·d the ruthless fate,
  That whelm 'd the *mystic* word.

At length through time's expanded sphere,
  Fair Science speeds her way,
And warm 'd by truth's refulgence clear,
  Reflects the kindred ray;
A second fabric's tow 'ring height
  Proclaims the *sign* restor 'd,
From whose foundation, brought to light,
  Is drawn the *mystic* word.

To depths obscure, the favor 'd Trine
  A dreary course engage,
Till through the Arch the ray divine
  Illumes the sacred page !
From the wide wonders of this blaze,
  Our ancient *sign 's* restor 'd,
The Royal Arch alone displays
  The long lost *mystic* word.

TEMPLAR'S SONGS.

40. HYMN.

Guide me, O thou great Jehovah!
  Pilgrim through this barren land :
I am weak but thou art mighty—
  Hold me in thy powerful hand ;
    Bread of heaven,
  Feed me till I want no more.

Open now thy crystal fountain,
  Whence the healing streams do flow.
Let the fiery, cloudy pillar,
  Lead me all my journey through ;
    Strong deliv'rer,
  Be thou still my strength and shield.

Feed me with the heav'nly manna,
  In this barren wilderness ;
Be my sword, and shield, and banner,
  Be my robe of righteousness ;
    Fight and conquor
  All my foes by sovereign grace.

When I tread the verge of Jordan,
  Bid my anxious fears subside ;
Foe to death and hell's destruction,
  Land me safe on Canaan's side ;
    Songs of praises
  I will ever give to thee.

41. SONG.

As, when the weary trav'ler gains
  the hight of some commanding hill,
His heart revives, if o'er the plains
  He sees his home, though distant still;

So, when the Christian pilgrim views
  By faith his mansion in the skies,
The sight his fainting strength renews,
  And wings his speed to reach the prize.

The hope of heaven his spirit cheers;
  No more he grieves for sorrows past:
Nor any future conflict fears,
  So he may safe arrive at last.

O Lord on thee our hopes we stay,
  To lead us on to thine abode;
Assur'd thy love will far oer'pay
  The hardest labors of the road.

42. SONG.

He dies, the friend of   sin-ners dies! Lo!

Salem's daughters weep around, A solemn darkness
vails the skies, A sudden trembling shakes the ground

Come, saints, and drop a tear or two
　For him who groan'd 'beneath your load,
He shed a thousand drops for you,
　A thousand drops of richer blood.

Here's love and grief beyond degree,
　The Lord of glory dies for man!
But lo! what sudden joys we see:
　Jesus, the dead, revives again!

The rising God forsakes the tomb;
　(In vain the tomb forbids his rise,)
Cherubic legions guard him home,
　And shout him "Welcome to the skies!"

Break off your tears, ye saints, and tell
　How high your great Deliverer reigns;
Sing how he spoil'd the hosts of hell,
　And lead the monster death in chains!

Say "Live forever wond'rous King!
  Born to redeem, and strong to save!"
Then ask the monster, "Where's thy sting?"
  And "Where's thy victory, boasting grave?"

43. SONG.

Angels! roll the rock away! Death yield up thy

'Tis the Savior—Seraphs, raise Your triumphant

Lift, ye saints—lift up your eyes! Now to glory

mighty prey ! See ! He ri - ses   from the tomb,

shouts of praise ; Let the earth's remotest   bound

see Him rise ! Hosts of angels   on   the   road,

Ri - ses with im - mor - tal   bloom.

Hear   the   joy in - spir - ing   sound.

Hail   and   sing th' in - car - nate   God.

Ri - ses with im - mor - tal bloom.

Hear the joy in - spir - ing sound.

Hail and sing th'in - car - nate God.

Heaven unfolds its portals wide ;
Gracious conqueror through them ride,
King of glory ! mount thy throne,
Boundless empire is thine own.

Praise him, all ye heavenly choirs,
Praise and sweep your golden lyres ;
Praise him in the noblest songs ;
Praise him from ten thousand tongues.

LAYING A FOUNDATION STONE.

44. HYMN.

To Heaven's high Architect all praise,
  All gratitude be given,
Who deign'd the human soul to raise
  By secrets sprung from Heaven.
    Then sound the great Jehovah's praise;
    To Him the glorious structure raise.

Now swells the choir in solemn tone,
  And hovering *angels* join;
Religion looks delighted down,
  When vot'ries press the shrine.

Blest be the place! thither repair
  The *true* and *pious* train:
Devotion wakes her anthems there,
  And heaven accepts the strain.

---

45. SONS OF A GLORIOUS ORDER.

Sons of a glo - ri - ous or - der anointed To cher - ish for a - ges the

ark of the Lord, Wearing the mys-ti-cal

badges ap-point-ed, Come to the tem-ple with

sweetest ac - cord. Come lay the corner stone

Asking the Lord to own Labors that

'tend to his glo - ry and praise; Long may the

mercy seat, Where angels' pinions meet,

Rest in the beau - ti - ful tem - ple ye raise.

CHORUS in last stanza, observing small notes, swell, and hold.

Brothers united, to you it is given,
To enlighten the woes of a sin-blighted world,
Far o 'er the earth, on the free winds of heaven,
Now let your banners of love be unfurled.
Write there the blessed three,
Faith, Hope, and Charity,
Names that shall live through the cycle of time,
Write them on every heart,
Make them your guide and chart,
Over life's sea to the heavens sublime.

Go forth befriending the way-weary stranger,
  Bright'ning the pathway that sorrow hath cross'd;
Strength'ning the weak, in the dark hour of danger,
  Clothing the naked and seeking the lost.
      Opening the prison door,
      Feeding the starving poor,
  Chiding the evil, approving the just,
      Drying the widow's tears,
      Soothing the orphan's fears,
  Great is your mission, in " God is your trust."

Go, in the spirit of him who is holy,
  Gladden the wastes and the by-ways of earth,
Visit the homes of the wretched and lowly,
  Bringing relief to the desolate hearth.
      Bind up the broken heart,
      Joy to the sad impart,
  Stay the oppressor and strengthen the just;
      Freely do ye receive,
      Freely to others give,
  Great is your mission, in "God is your trust."

FOR INSTALLATION.

46. HYMN.

First Voice. Andante.

'Let there be light!' th' Almighty spoke!

Second Voice.

' Let there be light th' Almighty spoke !

Bass.

Re - ful - gent streams from chaos broke,

Re - ful - gent streams from chaos broke,

T'il - lume the ris - ing earth

T' il - lume the ris - ing earth!

Well pleas'd the great Je - ho - vah stood,

Well pleas'd the great Je - ho - vah stood,

The Pow'r su - preme pro - nounc'd it good,

The Pow'r su - preme pro - nounc'd it good,

For.

And   gave   the   planets   birth !

And   gave   the   planets   birth !

CHORUS.

In   cho - ral num - bers   Masons join,

In   cho - ral num bers   Masons join,

To   bless   and praise this   Light Divine !

To   bless   and praise this   Light Divine !

Repeat the last Chorus.

Parent of light accept our praise,
Who shed'st on us thy brightest rays,
The light that fills the mind;
By choice selected, lo! we stand,
By friendship join'd a social band,
That love, that aid mankind.
CHORUS—In choral, &c.

The widow's tear, the orphan's cry,
All wants our ready hands supply,
As far as pow'r is giv'n;
The naked clothe, the pris'ner free,
These are thy works, sweet Charity;
Reveal'd to us from Heav'n.
CHORUS—In choral, &c.

DEDICATION OF HALLS.

47. SONG.

Hail, u - ni - versal Lord! By heav'n and

Hail, u - ni - versal Lord! By heav'n and

earth a - dor 'd, All hail, Great God! Before thy

earth a - dor 'd, All hail, Great God! Before thy

throne we bend,   To us thy grace extend, And

throne we bend,   To us thy grace extend, And

to our pray 'r attend! All   hail, Great God!

to our pray 'r attend! All   hail, Great God!

O, hear our pray 'r to day,
Turn not thy face away;
O Lord, our God!

Heav 'n, thy dread dwelling-place,
Can not contain thy Grace,
Remember now our race,
    O Lord, our God !

God of our fathers hear,
And to our cry be near,
    Jehovah, God !
The Heav 'ns eternal bow,
Forgive in mercy now
Thy suppliants here, O thou,
    Jehovah God !

To thee our hearts do draw,
On them O write thy law,
    Our Saviour, God !
When in this Lodge we 're met,
And at thine altar knelt,
O, do not us forget,
    Our Saviour, God !

---

48. ODE.

ALMIGHTY FATHER ! God of Love !
    Sacred, eternal king of kings !
From thy celestial courts above,
    Send beams of grace on seraph's wings ;
O, may they, gilt with light divine,
    Shed on our hearts inspiring rays ;
While, bending at this sacred shrine,
    We offer mystic songs of praise.

Faith ! with divine and heav 'nward eye,
    Pointing to radiant realms of bliss,
Shed here thy sweet benignity,
    And crown our works with happiness ;

Hope! too, with bosom void of fear,
　Still on thy steadfast anchor lean,
O, shed thy balmy influence here,
　And fill our breasts with joy serene.

And thou, fair Charity! whose smile
　Can bid the heart forget its woe,
Whose hand can misery's care beguile,
　And kindness' sweetest boon bestow,
Here shed thy sweet, soul-soothing ray;
　Soften our hearts, thou Pow'r divine!
Bid the warm gem of pity play,
　With sparkling luster, on our shrine.

Thou, who art thron'd 'midst dazzling light,
　And wrapp'd in brilliant robes of gold,
Whose flowing locks of silv'ry white
　Thy age and honor both unfold,
Genius of Masonry! descend,
　And guide our steps by thy strict law;
O, swiftly to our temple bend,
　And fill our breasts with solemn awe.

49.　HYMN.

GREAT source of light and love,
　To thee our songs we raise;
O, in thy temple, Lord, above,
　Hear and accept our praise.

Shine on this festive day,
　Succeed its hop'd design:
And may our Charity display
　A love resembling thine.

May this fraternal band,
Now consecrated, bless 'd,
In Union all distinguish 'd stand,
In Purity be dress 'd.

May all the sons of peace,
Their ev 'ry grace improve;
Till discord thro' the nations cease,
And all the world be Love.

---

50. O D E.

Brothers re - joice!   for our task is com-pleted,

After the pattern ap - pointed of yore; Let the re-

ward to the Craftsmen be meted, While, with thanksgiving, we bow and adore; Low at the feet of Him,

Throned were the Ser - a - phim And the Archangels   sing anthems of   praise : Born of the

lowly dust,   Wanting in faith and trust, How shall we

worship Thee,　Ancient　of　days?

Darkly we grope through the twilight of being;
　Weary we wait for the day dawning bright,
Father Omnific, Supreme and All-seeing,
　Come to thy Temple and fill it with Light.
　　Write here thy great New Name,
　　Kindle the altar flame,
Sacred to Thee, in the most holy place;
　　And where the cherubs fling
　　Light from each golden wing,
Leave us the Ark with its Symbols of grace.

Show us the Truth and the pathway of duty;
　Help us to lift up our standard sublime,
'Til earth is restored to the Order and Beauty
　Lost in the shadowless morning of Time.
　　Teach us to sow the seed
　　Of many a noble deed;

Make us determined, unflinching, and strong —
    Armed with the sword of right,
    Dauntless, amid the fight,
Help us to Level the bulwarks of wrong.

Prompt us to labor, as Thou hast directed,
  On the foundation laid sure in the past;
And may "the Stone which the builders rejected,"
  Crown our endeavors with glory at last.
        Then, at the eventide,
        Laying the Square aside,
May we look calmly on life's setting sun;
        And at the Mercy Seat,
        Where ransomed spirits meet,
Hear from the Master the plaudit "well done."

FUNERAL OCCASIONS.

51. HYMN.

Thou art gone to the grave, but we

Thou art gone to the grave, we no

Thou art gone to the grave, and its

Thou art gone to the grave, but 't were

will not deplore thee, Tho' sorrow and darkness en-

longer behold thee, Nor tread the rough path of the

mansions forsaken,   Perhaps thy tried spirit in

wrong to deplore thee, When God was thy ransom, thy

compass the tomb, The Savior has passed thro' its

world by thy side ; But the wide arms of mercy are

doubt lingered long ; But the sunshine of heaven beamed

guardian and guide ; He gave thee, and took thee, and

portals be - fore thee, And the lamp of his

spread to en - fold thee, And sinners may

bright on thy waking, And the song that thou

soon will re - store thee, Where death hath no

love is thy guide through the gloom, And the

hope since the Savior hath died, And

heardst was the seraphim's song, And

sting, since the Savior hath died, Where

lamp of his love is thy guide thro' the gloom.

sinners may hope since the Savior hath died.

song that thou heardst was the seraphim's song.

death hath no sting, since the Savior hath died.

52. ODE.

Oh! breathe not his name, let it sleep in the shade,
Where cold and unhonor'd his relics are laid;
Sad, silent, and dark be the tears that we shed,
As the night dew that falls on the grass o 'er his
     head!

But the night dew that falls, tho' in silence it weeps,
Shall brighten with verdure the grave where he
     sleeps;
And the tear that we shed tho' in secret it rolls,
Shall long keep his memory green in our souls.

53. HYMN.

Adagio.

Unveil   thy   bosom,   faith - ful

Unveil   thy   bosom,   faith - ful

tomb,   Take this new   treasure   to

tomb,   Take this new   treasure   to

thy   trust,   And   give these   sacred

thy   trust,   And   give these   sacred

relics room To slum - ber in

relics room To slum - ber in

the si - lent dust, And give these

the si - lent dust, And give these

sa - cred rel - ics room To slum-

sa - cred rel - ics room To slumber in the si - lent dust.

ber in the si - lent dust.

Nor pain, nor grief, nor anxious fear,
Invade thy bounds; no mortal woes
Can reach the silent sleepers here,
And angels watch their soft repose.

So Jesus slept; God's dying Son,
Past through the grave, and blest the bed;
Rest here dear Saint, 'til from his throne
The morning break, and pierce the shade.

Break from his throne, illustr'ous morn,
Attend, O Earth, his sov'reign word;
Restore thy trust, a glorious form,
He must ascend to meet his Lord.

---

54. FUNERAL HYMN.

"Man dieth and wasteth away,
  And where is he?"—Hark! from the skies,
I hear a voice answer, and say
  "The spirit of man never dies:

His body which came from the earth,
　　Must mingle again with the sod;
But his soul, which in heaven had birth,
　　Returns to the bosom of God."

The sky will be burnt as a scroll,
　　The earth, wrapt in flames, will expire;
But, freed from all shackles, the soul
　　Will rise in the midst of the fire.
Then, brothers, mourn not for the dead
　　Who rest from their labors, forgiven:
Learn this from your bible instead,
　　The grave is the gate-way to heaven.

Oh Lord God Almighty! to Thee
　　We turn as our solace above;
The waters may fail from the sea,
　　But not from thy fountains of love:
O teach us Thy will to obey,
　　And sing with one heart and accord,
"The Lord gives and the Lord takes away,
　　And praised be the name of the Lord."

ANNIVERSARIES.

55. OF ST. JOHN THE BAPTIST.

Ah, who that ne - ver felt can know, How

Ah, who that ne - ver felt can know, How

heavy hangs the day, When all the heart holds

heavy hangs the day, When all the heart holds

MELODIES

For.

dear below Is absent far a - way. Ah,

dear below Is absent far a - way. Ah,

who, that never felt, can tell How swiftly flies the

who, that never felt, can tell How swiftly flies the

hour, Which at last, Dangers past, Brings back

hour, Which at last, Dangers past, Brings back

joys, with'ring fast, Life's a sky, o - ver

joys, with'ring fast, Life's a sky, o - ver

Life's a sky,

cast, Sunbeams play or tempests low'r. Life's a

cast, Sunbeams play or tempests low'r. Life's a

overcast, sunbeams play or tempests low'r.

sky, o - ver-cast, Sunbeams play or tempests

sky, o - ver-cast, Sunbeams play or tempests

low'r, Sunbeams play or tempests low'r.

low'r, Sunbeams play or tempests low'r.

Many a weary sun had set,
   Ere thine, St. John, arose ;
Many an eye must still be wet,
   Before the day shall close :
O, may we on thy natal day
Thy sainted spirit feel,
    Dry the eye,
    Hush the sigh
Of the low and the high ;
Sorrow's dart no one may fly,
   But its wound our Art can heal.

The sigh, tho' hush'd, the tear, though dried,
   Though sorrow pain no more ;
Yet poor 's the bliss to earth allied,
   When earthly scenes are o'er :
But heav 'n descended Masonry
   Th' immortal world unveils ;
    There decay,
    Old and gray,
With no ruin marks his way ;
There shall Virtue safely stay,
   Heav 'n ne 'er promises and fails.

56. FESTIVAL OF ST. JOHN.

WHEN chaos invested the face of the deep,
And to darkness, confusion and discord gave birth,
The fiat of heaven mid the tumult was heard,
And nature obey'd the omnipotent word.
Jehovah's great mandate was, 'Let there be light ;'
And harmony triumph'd o'er discord and night.

What joy fill'd the earth, when the herald of love,
On a mission of mercy dispatch'd from above,
While the choir of high heaven reecho'd the strain,
Proclaim'd 'On earth, peace and good will toward men;'
What raptures ecstatic, were born on the sound,
That spread the glad tidings creation around.

Thus the moral world joy'd, when the shadows of night
Were chas'd from the soul by effulgence of Light ;
When by Wisdom contriv'd, and in Beauty array'd,
And by strength well supported, our Lodge stood dis-
      play'd ;
With the 'Olive of Peace' Freemasonry rose,
And dissention was hush'd on the breast of repose.

To perform to acceptance we 're ever inclin'd,
Our duty to God, to ourselves and mankind ;
Thus our course through this life of probation we steer,
And when Scripture we follow, no danger we fear ;
Our square and our compass are ne 'er misapplied,
Our trust is in God — and his *word* is our guide.

The passage of life to convey us safe o 'er,
While we pray for the breeze, let us ply at the oar ;
To the Grand Lodge in heaven for admission we pray,
And *Faith*, *Hope* and *Charity* point out the way ;
To that blest consummation we press gladly on,
And take for our Model, our *Patron*, St. John.

Then in prayer Masons join, to our *Master* above,
That our lodges on earth may be lodges of love ;
That the whole race of man may hereafter be blest,
Through Eternity's day in the mansions of rest ;
Then shout, Brethren, shout in harmonious glee,
In unison shout the meet — ' So mote it be.'

MEETING OF A GRAND LODGE.

57. SONG.

Hail, to the day! when assembled in union,
Springs at the altar of Friendship and Truth, Pledge
of our fairest, our dear - est communion, The flow-
'ret, which blooms in pe - ren-ni-al youth, Hail to the
day! when assembled in Union, Springs at the altar of Friendship and Truth, Pledge of our fairest, our
dearest communion, The flow'ret, which blooms in pe-

Allegro. Moderato.

ren-ni-al youth; E'er has it flourish'd fair,

Sigh'd on by heav'n's air, Nurtur'd by dew drops, dis-

till'd from a - bove Bright o'er its natal bed,

Beams of gay light shall spread, Strength'ning the rays

of *Af - fec - tion* and *Love.*

Hail to the Craft! whose light, broadly beaming,
   Streams from the lovliest *Star* of the sky;
O 'er sorrows vale ever cheerfully gleaming,
   Guiding to yonder bright temple on high;
      Still may that holy ray,
      Type of Immortal day,
Light the lone path of the pilgrim along;
      'Till the Grand Master's 'hest
      Bid all his labors rest,
Attuning his harp to the mystical song.

Long may each Mason be firm in his duty,
   The grand and the useful in harmony join;
Long in his Temple may Wisdom and Beauty,
   Stars of the high arch of Masonry, shine;

Here may we often meet
Each brother true to greet,
Time strewing flow'rs o'er the swift rolling year;
Here may fair Union rise
Here join the good and wise,
Charity, Friendship, and Truth to revere.

Now to Creation's Great Builder ascending,
Loud let the Chorus of Gratitude swell;
Here as before him we humbly are bending,
O! may He deign in his Temple to dwell;
Here may the social fire
Of love to heav'n aspire,
Long from this Altar rise Incense of praise
To the Eternal One,
Our ceaseless shining sun,
Master of All— Holy, "Ancient of Days!"

---

58. SONG.

FROM envy, strife, and pride;
From all the sorrow, weariness, and care,
That Heaven permits our human hearts to bear,
Now let us turn aside.

We meet, as met the good,
When first our glorious jewels were enshrined —
Time has no power to break the ties that bind
Our mystic brotherhood.

Like some resplendant star,
Above the somber clouds of Pagan night,
In radiant beauty rose Masonic light,
And cast its beams afar.

And still in every clime,
Above the sneer of scorn, the frown of hate,
Revered and cherished by the good and great,
Our Order stands sublime.

When ages have gone by,
Still it will flourish in immortal youth —
Faith may be lost in sight, but love and truth
Can never, never die.

Here warring passions cease ;
Here from the turmoils of the world apart,
The weary spirit and the bleeding heart
Find comfort, rest, and peace

Since last we met, dear friends,
Who clasped our hands and greeted us in love,
Have joined the Grand Triumphant Lodge above,
Whose meeting never ends.

Life's sands are falling fast ;
We know not when our hearts shall cease to beat —
This season of communion, calm and sweet,
May be on earth our last.

Hence, watching day by day,
Let us improve the talents God has given ;
He will require a strict account, when heaven
And earth shall pass away.

It is our task below,
To lead the wayward from the path of sin ;
To feed the hungry, take the stranger in,
And solace human woe.

To seek the poor abode ;
To minister beside the dying bed —
To soothe the suffering, hold the fainting head.
And point the soul to God.

Let us be firm and true,
Forgetting never the All-Seeing Eye,
Of Him who sits upon the throne on high,
Beholding all we do.

And when the sea and land
Shall render up to God their sleeping dust,
Through grace unmerited we humbly trust,
To meet at His right hand.

MISCELLANEOUS SONGS.

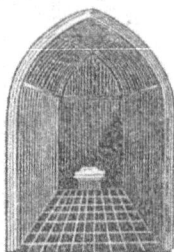

59. SONG.

AS SUNG AT THE FUNERAL OF WASHINGTON.

WHILE all our nation whelm 'd in grief,
Lament their General, Patriot, Chief,
Let us, his brethren, long revere
A name to Masonry so dear!

In mystic rites our Lodge displays,
Its sorrows and its patron's praise;
And spreads fresh garlands round the tomb,
Where the sweet cassia long shall bloom.

Look to the East; its splendors fail!
The lesser lights grow dim and pale!
The glory once reflected here
Now dawns upon a higher sphere!

60. SONG.

Not the fictions of Greece nor the dreams of old Rome,
Shall with visions mislead, or with meteors consume;
No Pegasus' wings my short soarings misguide,
Nor raptures detain me on Helicon's side.
All clouds now dissolve; from the east beams the day:
Truth rises in glory, and wakens the lay.
The eagle-ey'd muse—sees the light—fills the grove
With the song of Freemasons, of friendship and love!

Inspir'd with the theme, the divinity flies,
And thron'd on a rainbow—before her arise
Past, present, and future—with splendid array,
In Masonic succession, their treasures display:
She views murder'd merit by ruffian-hand fall,
And the grave give its dead up, at fellowship's call!
While the Craft, by their badges, their innocence prove;
And the song of Freemasons is friendship and love!

From those ages remote see the muse speeds her way,
To join in the glories the present display.
In freedom and friendship she sees the true band
With their splendor and virtues illumine the land.
Religion's pure beams break the vapors of night,
And from darkness mysterious the word gives the light!
While the lodge here below, as the choirs from above,
Join the song of Freemasons, in friendship and love!

That the future might keep what the present bestows,
In rapture prophetic the goddess arose;
As she sung through the skies, angels echo'd the sound,
And the winds bore the notes to the regions around;
The kind proclamation our song shall retain,
'T was—" That Masonry long may its luster maintain.
And till Time be no more, our fraternity prove,
That the objects we aim at, are friendship and love!"

61. SONG.

ON THE REVIVAL OF MASONRY.

WHEN Masonry expiring lay,
  By knaves and fools rejected,
Without one hope, one cheering ray,
  By worthless fools neglected;
    Fair Virtue fled,
    Truth hung her head,
O 'erwhelm 'd in deep confusion,
    Sweet Friendship too
    Her smiles withdrew
From this best institution.
    CHORUS. Fair Virtue fled, &c.

Columbia's sons determin 'd then
  Freemasonry to cherish;
They rous 'd her into life again,
  And bid fair science flourish.
    Now Virtue bright,
    Truth rob 'd in white,
With Friendship hither hastens;
    All go in hand
    To bless the band
Of upright faithful Masons.
    CHORUS. Now Virtue bright, &c.

Since Masonry's reviv 'd once more,
  Pursue her wise directions;
Let circumspection go before,
  And Virtue square your actions;
    Unite your hands
    In Friendship's bands,

Supporting one another;
　With honest heart
　Fair truth impart
To every faithful brother.
　　CHORUS.　Unite your hands, &c.

But may kind Heaven's gracious hand
　Still regulate each action;
May every lodge securely stand
　Against the storms of faction;
　　May Love and Peace
　　Each day increase
Throughout this happy nation;
　　May they extend
　　Till all shall end
In one great conflagration.
　　CHORUS.　May Love and peace, &c.

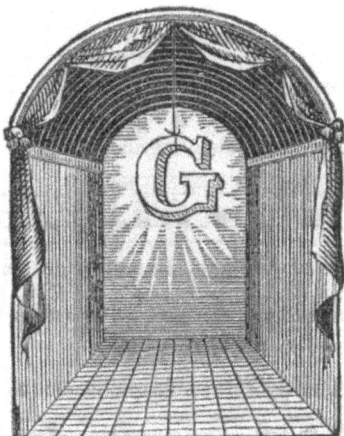

62. SONG.

Andantino.

Arise, and blow thy trumpet, Fame! Freemason-

Arise, and blow thy trumpet, Fame! Freemason-

Arise, and blow thy trumpet, Fame! Freemason-

ry aloud proclaim, To realms and worlds unknown;

ry aloud proclaim, To realms and worlds unknown;

ry aloud proclaim, To realms and worlds unknown;

Tell them 'twas this great David's son, The wise, the

Tell them 'twas this great David's son, The wise, the

Tell them 'twas this great David's son, The wise, the

matchless Solomon, Priz'd far above his throne.

matchless Solomon, Priz'd far above his throne.

matchless Solomon, Priz'd far above his throne.

The solemn temples, cloud-capt towers,
Th' aspiring domes, are works of ours,
By us those piles were rais'd;

Then bid mankind with songs advance,
And through th' ethereal vast expanse
   Let Masonry be prais'd!

We help the poor in time of need,
The naked clothe, the hungry feed,
   'Tis our foundation stone:
We build upon the noblest plan,
For friendship rivets man to man,
   And makes us all as one.

Still louder, Fame! thy trumpet blow;
Let all the distant regions know
   Freemasonry is this:
Almighty Wisdom gave it birth,
And Heav'n has fix'd it here on earth,
   A type of future bliss!

------

63. SONG.

WHAT is life of love bereft,
   When its heav'nly joys are fled?
Lives the heart that love has left,
   Is there life when love is dead?

When our ills were first fill'd up,
   Love the sweet'ning drop did give;
And by mingling in the cup,
   Made it worth man's while to live.

Sweetest passion, gen'rous flame,
   Parent of the tender sigh,
Let us praise thy honor'd name,
   By loving truly till we die.

64. SONG.

HUMANITY'S soft, gentle band
   Unites us to each other;
And ev'ry heart and ev'ry hand
   Should try to save a brother.
Not only should the kindred tie
   Incline us to be kind;
But ev'ry tear, that dims the eye,
   Should wound the feeling mind.

We're children of one family,
   And earth, our common mother;
When sorrow and distress we see,
   With joy relieve a brother.
Humanity! thou gift divine,
   The mind is cold and dark,
That will not to thy voice incline,
   Nor feel the pitying spark.

---

65. ODE.

REST, holy pilgrim, rest, I pray,
Dreary to Mecca's shrine thy way;
O deign an hermit's hut to share,
Nor proudly spurn his homely fare.

But say from whence thy sorrows flow,
Impart each secret source of woe;
For time, I see, and grief have spread
A silver halo o'er thy head.

No ruffian, lawless steps intrude
To blast the joys of solitude;

But peace and meditation dwell,
Sweet inmates of the hermit's cell.

To quench thy thirst the rock shall flow,
To feed thee, sweetest fruits shall grow,
Soft dreams shall nature's waste repair,
Then deign an hermit's hut to share.

———

66. HYMN.

O, CHARITY! thou heav'nly grace,
  All tender, soft and kind;
A friend to all the human race,
  To all, that's good and kind.
The man of charity extends
  To all his lib'ral hand;
His kindred, neighbors, foes and friends,
  His pity may command.

He aids the poor in their distress—
  He hears when they complain;
With tender heart delights to bless
  And lessen all their pain:
The sick, the prisoner, poor, and blind,
  And all the sons of grief,
In him a benefactor find,
  He loves to give relief.

'T is love, that makes religion sweet,
  'T is love, that makes us rise,
With willing mind and ardent feet,
  To yonder happy skies:
Then let us all in love abound,
  And Charity pursue;
Thus shall we be with glory crown'd,
  And love as angels do.

67. SONG.

How blest is he, whose gen 'rous soul
　　Will to the needy joy impart;
Who bids the streams of pity roll,
　　To cheer the helpless wand 'rer's heart.

Nor shall the widow's fervent prayer,
　　For him, unheeded, rise above,
But soar to heav 'nly regions fair,
　　And reach th' Eternal Throne of Love.

The houseless orphan, doom 'd to roam,
　　Shall oft repeat the Mason's name,
And when he leaves his shelt 'ring dome,
　　Through ev 'ry wand 'ring, tell his fame.

For him the matin song shall rise,
　　And evening vesper soft ascend,
Imploring God, who rules the skies,
　　To bless the child of sorrow's friend.

68. SONG.

WHEN the star of thy destiny glows,
　　With a brilliancy gilding thy days;
When the free hand of Providence throws
　　The roses of hope on thy ways;
When the world seems to pour at thy feet,
　　Its treasures in ne 'er-failing streams;
And thy hours, for such blisses to fleet,
　　Glide smoothly, as young lovers' dreams.

Let thy pleasure, reflected, be thrown
　　Mid the darkness of sorrow and care;

Make the cause of the widowed thine own,
　And thy wealth with the fatherless share.
Let thy footsteps bring joy to the ear
　Of the sorrowing children of pain;
And thy tongue proclaim succor is near,
　To those who 've long sought it in vain.

And despair shall not vanquish thy soul,
　When the clouds of adversity lower;
Nor the waters of misery roll
　O 'er thy spirit with mastering power.
For the pain thou hast helped to subdue,
　The anguish thy hand hath allayed,
Shall descend on thy spirit like dew,
　To refreshen — to solace — to aid.

---

69. SONG.

OH! think when misfortune has wither 'd the heart,
　How cheering a brother to find;
What blessings the voice of a friend can impart
　To the drooping disconsolate mind!
The hand grasped in friendship, diffuses a charm,
　Can smooth the deep furrows of care;
Can fate's stern decree of its terrors disarm,
　And banish the gloom of despair.
Can fate's stern decree of its terrors disarm,
　And banish the gloom of despair.

70. SONG.

SHOULD the chances of life ever tempt me to roam,
In a Lodge of Freemasons I'll still find a home;
There the sweet smile of friendship still welcomes
each guest,
And Brotherly love gives that welcome a zest.

When I'm absent from Lodge, pleasure tempts me
in vain,
As I sigh for the moments of meeting again;
For friendship and harmony truly are there,
Where we meet on the level and part on the square.

There the soul-binding Union surely is known,
Which unites both the peasant and prince on the
throne;
There the rich and the poor on the level do meet,
And, as brothers, each other most cordially greet.

On the quick sands of life should a brother be thrown,
It is then that the friendship of brothers is shown;
For the heart points the hand, his distress to remove,
For our motto is "Kindness and brotherly love."

When the master of all, from his star-studded throne,
Shall issue his mandate to summon us home;
May each brother be found, to be duly prepared,
In the Grand Lodge above us to meet his reward.

71. THE MASON'S PRAYER.

PARENT of all! Omnipotent
  In heav'n and earth below;
Through all creation's bounds unspent,
  Whose streams of goodness flow.

Teach me to know from whence I rose,
  And unto what design'd;
No private aims let me propose,
  Since link'd with human kind.

But chief to hear fair virtue's voice,
  May all my thoughts incline;
'Tis reason's law, 'tis wisdom's choice,
  'Tis nature's call and thine.

Me from our sacred order's cause,
  Let nothing e'er divide;
Grandeur, nor gold, nor vain applause,
  Nor friendship false misguide.

Teach me to feel a *brother's* grief,
  To do in all what's best;
To suff'ring man to give relief,
  And blessing to be blest.

---

72. SONG.

OH! Masonry, our hearts inspire,
And warm us with thy sacred fire;
Make us obedient to thy laws,
And zealous to support thy cause;
  For thou and virtue are the same,
  And only differ in the name.

Pluck narrow notions from the mind,
And plant the love of human kind.
Teach us to feel a brother's woe,
And feeling, comfort to bestow ;
 Let none, unheeded, draw the sigh,
 No grief unnotic'd pass us by.

Let swelling Pride a stranger be,
Our friend compos'd Humility.
Our hands let steady Justice guide,
And Temp'rance at our boards preside ;
 Let Secrecy our steps attend,
 And injur'd Worth our tongues defend.

Drive Meanness from us, sly Deceit,
And Calumny, and rigid Hate ;
Oh ! may our highest.pleasure be
To add to man's felicity :
 And may we, as thy votaries true,
 Thy paths, oh ! Masonry, pursue.

73. SONG.

O **what** a happy thing it is,
 "Brethren to dwell in unity !"
While ev'ry action's squar'd by this,
 The true base line of Masonry,
Our plumb-line fixed is the point,
 The angle of uprightness shows ;
From side to side, from joint to joint,
 By steps the stately mansion rose.

Whate'er the order or the plan,
 The parts will with the whole agree
For by a geometric man,
 The work is done in symmetry.

From east to west, from north to south,
 Far as the foaming billows roll,
Faith, Hope, and silver-braided Truth,
 Shall stamp with worth the Mason's soul.

But, chiefest, come, sweet Charity,
 Meek, tender, hospitable guest;
Aided by those, inspir'd by thee,
 How tranquil is the Mason's breast!
An olive branch thy forehead binds,
 The gift that peerless Prudence gave,
An emblem of congenial minds,
 And such Masonic brethren have.

---

74. SONG.

WHEN the sun from the east salutes mortal eyes,
And the sky-lark melodiously bids us arise;
With our hearts full of joy we the summons obey,
And haste to our work at the dawn of the day.

On the tressel our master draws angles and lines,
There with freedom and fervency forms his designs;
Not a picture on earth is so lovely to view,
All his lines are so perfect, his angles so true.

In the west see the wardens submissively stand,
The master to aid; and obey his command;
The intent of his signal we perfectly know,
And we ne'er take offense when he gives us a blow.

In the Lodge, sloth and dullness we always avoid,
Fellow-crafts and apprentices all are employ'd:
Perfect ashlers some finish, some make the rough plain,
All are pleas'd with their work, and are pleas'd
    with their gain.

75. SONG.

GRANT me, kind Heav'n, what I request,
In Masonry let me be blest;
Direct me to that happy place,
Where friendship smiles in every face;
Where freedom, and sweet innocence,
Enlarge the mind and cheer the sense.

Where sceptered reason from her throne,
Surveys the Lodge and makes us one;
And harmony's delightful sway
For ever sheds ambrosial day;
Where we blest Eden's pleasures taste,
While balmy joys are our repast.

Our Lodge the social virtues grace,
And wisdom's rule we foudly trace;
All nature, open'd to our view,
Points out the paths we should pursue;
Let us subsist in lasting peace,
And may our happiness increase.

---

76. SONG.

Three thousand years a - way have roll'd, since

that bright banner first was seen To   float in pride o'er

tents of old, Where worshipped Israel's wisest king,

A - round the old and   vine-clad hills, Where

Patriarchs and Prophets trod, It wav'd—near Judah's

murm'ring rills, And o'er the Temple built for God.

CHORUS —Our banners bright — Our banners bright,
We fling them out on freedom's air;
Our banners bright — Our banners bright,
Behold our beauteous EMBLEMS there.

That banner floated many a year,
Beneath the tempest's blasting wings;
But still it proudly flutters here,
And still around our hearts it clings.
'Mong *ruins deep* o'er *rugged ways*,
Beneath its folds, in *Pilgrim garb*,
We labored oft, in other days,
To gain the *long lost mystic word*.

CHORUS—Our banners bright—Our banners bright, &c.

Hail, noble Flag! the loved and *free*,
Around thee, gathering, still shall meet
As erst, in bonds of Masonry,
And Brother, fondly, Brother greet.
And when we've *marked* our last *design*,
And *passed* as Pilgrims to the grave,
That Flag shall still in glory shine,
And o'er our slumbers gently wave.

CHORUS—- Our banners bright—Our banners bright, &c.

77. SONG.

FAITH, HOPE, AND CHARITY.

Faith.

There's a vision once seen never passeth from sight,
For it fixeth the eye, fills the soul with delight;
It clears all obstructions, admits of no shade,
Is a light to the mind — 't is a beam not to fade.

Hope.

There's a glow so seraphic, to gladden the earth,
We feel, while it lingers, its heavenly birth,
It blesses and cheers, soothes and comforts the world,
Embracing the globe, with its bright folds unfurl 'd.

Charity.

There's a joy so absorbing, a rapture so calm,
It lives while there's impulse the heart's blood to warm,
Nor quenched till the spirit shall part from the clay,
It illumes with its glory life's dreariest day.

78. THE MASON'S BRIDE.

A clear bell sounds upon the breeze, And lo! a bridal

train Is winding through the forest trees To yonder

sa - cred fane; And there, before the chancel rail, Two

hearts de - vo - ted bow, The Pride and Beauty

of the vale, Ex - change the nuptial vow: And

now, 'mid many a beaming smile, The lov 'd one by her

side, She passes down the echo - ing aisle, A

youth - ful Ma - son's bride.

Away, along the thundering main
  A gallant vessel flies,
Like war-steed o 'er the battle plain,
  Or lightning through the skies ;
And far behind, a line of blue
  Between the sky and sea,
Her native land fades on her view
  In dim obscurity.
"Ah! from the true and tried I rove,"
  The weeping lady cried,
A kind voice whisper 'd, " Gentle love,
  Thou art a Mason's Bride.

And fear thee not, in every land
  Beneath yon sky of blue,
Thou 'lt meet a warm, devoted band
  Of Brothers — kind and true.
And ne 'er the world's tempestuous war
  Their noble bark shall 'whelm,
While Faith shall be their guiding star,
  And Love directs the helm.
Then fear thee not where 'er we rove,
  Whatever ills betide,
"Remember, yes, remember love,
  Thou art a Mason's Bride."

Ere long within a foreign land
  Health's lovely roses fled,
And sickness laid her blighting hand
  On that young lover's head.
And then, when at the mystic sign,
  Kind brothers round him press 'd,
And pour 'd sweet sympathy's pure wine
  Upon the stranger's breast —
And bade him on his journey speed
  With every want supplied —
That lady felt 't was blest indeed
  To be a Mason's Bride.

79. THE MASON AT MONTEREY.

The lurid sun hung low and red, Above the

plains of Monterey, Where, 'mong the dying and the

dead, A young and wounded soldier lay; Still from the

cannon's iron throat
Hoarse thunder burst, and gleaming flame, And blended

with the bugle's note, The far-off shout of triumph came.

But heeded not that shout of pride,
    The soldier stretch'd upon the plain,
For ooz'd away life's purple tide,
    And fever burn'd in ev'ry vein;
His thoughts were in his native land,
    Among the friends he held most dear,
Again he felt the breezes bland,
    And saw the waters gliding clear.

"Alas!" he sighed, "delicious dream,
  Those scenes shall never greet me more:
O for one draught from that sweet stream
  That sings beside my father's door."
Just then a Mason passing by,
  By the sweet angel Mercy sent,
Caught the poor youth's desponding sigh,
  And listened to his sad lament.

He brought him water bright and clear,
  And bound with skill each bleeding wound,
Then bore him on his breast sincere,
  Far from that bloody battle-ground.
Long Death and Life together strove,
  And oft Life's lamp burned dim and low,
But in his faithful work of love
  Ne'er did the Mason weary grow.

He marked with deep, intense delight,
  Health smile upon the grateful youth,
And heard him bless that Order bright
  Whose lovely "guiding-star is Truth."
That Order, whose pure sons are found
  Where'er the foot of man may rove —
Still pouring richest blessings round —
  The ministers of peace and love!

---

80. GEORGE WASHINGTON.

THERE's a Star in the West that shall never go down
  Till the records of valor decay;
We must worship its light, though it is not our own,
  For Liberty bursts in its ray;

Shall the name of a Washington ever be heard
   By a freeman, and thrill not his breast?
Is there one out of bondage that hails not the word
   As the Bethlehem Star of the West?

"War, war to the knife; be enthrall'd, or ye die!"
   Was the echo that woke in the land;
But it was not his voice that had prompted the cry,
   Nor his anger that kindled the brand;
He raised not his arm, he defied not his foes,
   While a leaf of the olive remain'd,
Till goaded with insult, his spirit arose
   Like a long-baited lion enchain'd.

He struck with firm courage the blow of the brave,
   But sigh'd for the carnage that spread;
He indignantly trampled the yoke of the slave,
   But wept for the thousands that bled.
Tho' he threw back the fetters and headed the strife
   Till man's charter was fairly restor'd,
Yet he prayed for the moment when freedom and life
   Should no longer be press'd by the sword.

Oh! his laurels were pure, and his patriot name
   In the page of the future shall dwell;
And be seen in the annals the foremost in fame,
   By the side of a Hoffer and Tell.
Revile not my song; for the wise and the good,
   Among Britons, have nobly confess'd
That his was the glory, and ours was the blood
   Of the deeply-stain'd field of the West.

81.
THERE IS MASONRY EVERYWHERE.

On the broad arch'd sky, when the queen of night Goes

forth in her robes of peer - less

white ; Or the sun breaks out from his gold - en

shroud, When the storm has pass'd on the

thunder - cloud ; 'Mid the star - ry host, when they

wan - der forth, As sen - ti - nels

bright o'er the sleep - ing earth ; Where the comets

wander through fields of air, On their lone - ly

rounds — there is Masonry there — there is Masonry there.

Abroad on the waves of the deep blue sea,
Where the tempests sport in the wildest glee ;
And the wild Albatross in its far-off home,
Like a storm-king sits on the wide sea-foam :
Or the placid waves of the rolling deep
Have quieted down in their summer's sleep,
And the seaman, calm 'd near the tropic's glare,
Woos the cooling breeze — *there is Masonry there.*

In the curtained halls of the lofty lord,
Where the jewels and wealth of the world are stored,
In the poor man's cot by some silent stream
Where the wild-wood stands in its spreading green :
On the mountains brow — in the valley deep —
In the throbbing pulse, or on beauty's cheek —
In the insect's home — in the lion's lair —
On the earth, sea, or sky — *there is Masonry there.*

TESTIMONIALS.

From the Grand Lodge of Indiana.

The Committee to whom was referred the examination of 'THE CRAFTSMAN AND FREEMASON'S GUIDE, containing a delineation of the Rituals of Freemasonry, from the Degree of Entered Apprentice to that of Select Master and the Order of Priesthood,' beg leave to report—that they have given the same a careful examination, and find it, in their opinion, to be one of the best Masonic Manuals yet published. It possesses not only the recommendation of being as brief in its delineations as it is possible, in order to convey the necessary amount of masonic instruction, but it is entirely divested of those crude and imperfect historical digests of the Institution, with which most editors of masonic Text-books, have incumbered the literature of the Craft. This may be, by some, considered as a great omission, but in our opinion it is one demanded by the increasing light of masonic intelligence. The work merely professes to be a Freemason's Guide, and, in our opinion, to the practical Mason, it contains all the elements of a true directory. We not only take pleasure, therefore, in commending the present compilation, by Brother Cornelius Moore, to this Grand Lodge, and the brethren in Indiana, but to the fraternity at large, as, in the estimation of your committee, it is the most valuable compilation for practical purposes that has yet been presented to our consideration.

C. SCMIDLAPP,
D. P. HOLLOWAY,
LEWIS BURK."

From the Grand Lodge of Kentucky.

Resolved, That this Grand Lodge recommend to the Fraternity of Freemasons, the "CRAFTSMAN," by Bro. C. Moore, as a work of much merit, and a very excellent pocket companion, and of great utility in conferring degrees by the Lodges.

From the Grand Lodge of Ohio.

The Select Committee appointed to examine and report upon the merits of "THE CRAFTSMAN," a work compiled and arranged by Bro. CORNELIUS MOORE, and published by Bro. JACOB ERNST, at Cincinnati, having examined the same, report:—

That they find it to be judiciously arranged and in proper order—the language correct and expressive, the symbols rightly disposed, and the price so reasonable as to bring it within the reach of every Mason. The committee offer for adoption the following resolution:

Resolved, That the Grand Lodge of Ohio approve of the Craftsman, and recommend it to be used by the Lodges subordinate to this Grand Lodge.

Respectfully submitted,

WILLIAM FIELDING,
M. Z. KREIDER,
W. B. SMITH.

WASHINGTON, Hempstead Co., Ark.,
June 7th, 1850

I have to some extent carefully examined "THE CRAFTSMAN AND FREE-MASON'S GUIDE," published by Bro. Jacob Ernst, of Cincinnati, Ohio, and observe with much pleasure and gratification its practical application. Its arrangement is excellent, and well calculated to facilitate greatly the explanation of the important lessons of the Order, easily directing the mind into a plain channel of masonic information. With these impressions I should rejoice to see its extended circulation, until it should be in the possession of every member of the craft in my own beloved Arkansas.

BENJ. P. JETT, P. G. M. of Ark.

ARKADELPHIA LODGE, No. 19.

WHEREAS, Brother Samuel Reed has introduced to our notice a work entitled "THE CRAFTSMAN AND FREEMASON'S GUIDE," published by Brother Jacob Ernst, which has received a cursory examination, and meets the wishes and desires of the fraternity at this place;

Therefore be it Resolved, That we, believing it to be the very best working book which has come under our observation, most cordially recommend it to the favorable consideration of the craft.

Be it further Resolved, That the Compiler, Brother Moore, and Brother Jacob Ernst, the publisher, deserve the gratitude of the fraternity for presenting a work possessed of such advantages.

H. FLANAGIN,
W. M. BRICE,   } Committee.
JAS. H. OBAUGH,

LITTLE ROCK, Ark., June 17th 1850.

On a careful examination of the "CRAFTSMAN," I give to it a most hearty approval, as the best working book I have seen. It is better arranged than Cross' Chart ; and contains in addition to the matter of that Chart, that most valuable of all masonic writings, the ANCIENT CONSTITUTIONS. It is much superior in arrangement to the TRESTLE BOARD, and adheres more closely in its text to the approved standard works.   E. H. ENGLISH.

THE TEMPLAR'S TEXT BOOK,---

Or Ritual of a Council of Knights of the Red Cross, and of an Encampment of Knights Templars, and Knights of Malta. Abridged from standard authors, by CORNELIUS MOORE, of Reed Encampment, No. 6, Ohio.

Morocco, marble edge,	50
Morocco tuck, gilt edge,	75

DIPLOMAS,---

Beautifully engraved Master Masons' and Royal Arch Diplomas, 16 by 20 inches in size, on Paper and Parchment, for framing : also printed on bank note paper, and neatly put up in map form.

MASTER MASONS' AND ROYAL ARCH DIPLOMAS--

On Parchment,	1 00
On Paper, Map form,	50

COUNCIL DIPLOMAS---

On Parchment,	1 00
On Paper, Map Form,	50

ENCAMPMENT DIPLOMAS---

On Parchment,	1 50
On Paper, or Map from,	75

Featured Titles from Westphalia Press

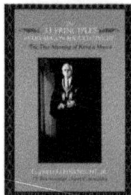

The 33 Principles Every Mason Should Live By: The True Meaning of Being a Mason by C. Fred Kleinknecht Jr.

These 33 principles are what all Freemasons should live by, they are the true meaning of Freemasonry. This book will not only benefit the Freemason but everyone can profit. I pass this along to you as a record of the Kleinknecht legacy of leadership.

Freemasonry, Politics and Rijeka (Fiume) (1785-1944) by Ljubinka Toseva Karpowicz

The greater part of the work concentrates on the efforts of Italian Irredentism in Rijeka in which intellectuals and Masons from Rijeka and Italy played a leading role. Some chapters analyze the work of Italian Masonry during the Fascist era, the military coup against the Free State of Fiume and much more.

Getting the Third Degree: Fraternalism, Freemasonry and History Edited by Guillermo De Los Reyes and Paul Rich

As this engaging collection demonstrates, the doors being opened on the subject range from art history to political science to anthropology, as well as gender studies, sociology and more. The organizations discussed may insist on secrecy, but the research into them belies that.

Dudley Wright: Writer, Truthseeker & Freemason by John Belton

Dudley Wright (1868-1950) was an Englishman who took a universalist approach to the various great Truths of Life, he travelled though many religions in his life and wrote about them all, but was probably most at home with Islam. As a professional journalist he made his living where he could.

Secrets & Lies in the United Kingdom: Analysis of Political Corruption Edited by Fabienne Portier-Le Cocq

Secrets & Lies in the United Kingdom: Analysis of Political Corruption lifts the shroud of secrecy in the United Kingdom in relation to modern freemasonry in Scotland in the late-18th century, the 'Stolen Generations' in Australia from the early 1900s to the late 1970s, and so much more.

An Introduction to the Formation of Freemasonry in the United States of America: The Constellation of the Brotherhood
by Larissa P. Watkins

The Constellation of the Brotherhood is another stellar reference resource by bibliographer Larissa Watkins. It encompasses the developmental history of the Grand Masonic Bodies in the United States for each state. It will be a boon to researchers, Masonic libraries as well as public and university libraries and others.

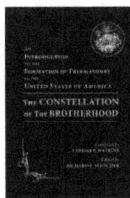

History of Freemasonry in the State of New York
by Ossian Lang

Social history as a corrective to a historiography is often too limited to diplomacy and wars. It began an upward trajectory as early as the 1930s, but it remains constrained by the frustrating cost and availability of materials that even great research libraries lack. This volume is a case in point.

Between Conflict and Conformity:: Freemasonry During the Weimar Republic and the "Third Reich"
by Ralf Melzer, Translated by Glenys A. Waldman

Freemasonry during the Weimar Republic and the 'Third Reich'... One might ask, "Is that a chapter of forgotten persecution or a legend of persecution?" After extensive research in archives in Berlin, Moscow, and Washington, D.C., the author has determined that the answer would have to be: "Neither, nor; yet some of both."

Chains of Empire: English Public Schools, Masonic Children, Historical Causality, and Imperial Clubdom

The British Empire's and the English public schools' peculiar system of rituals and rewards had more in common than has been realized. In Chains of Empire, Paul Rich related this to controversies about historical causality, morphic resonance, chaos, and the claims to influence of other bastions of the Imperial ethos.

Freemasonry: A French View
by Roger Dachez and Alain Bauer

Perhaps one should speak not of Freemasonry but of Freemasonries in the plural. In each country Masonic historiography has developed uniqueness, but it is safe to say that one of the highest levels of scholarship has been in France. This book is a case in point, as two of the best known French Masonic scholars present their own view of the worldwide evolution and challenging mysteries of the fraternity over the centuries.